DATE DUE			

Helga Fritzsch

Rabbits

Everything about Purchase, Care,
Nutrition, and Diseases

With 21 Color Photos by Outstanding Animal
Photographers and 32 Drawings by Fritz W. Köhler

Translated by Helgard Niewisch, D.V.M.

Barron's
Woodbury, New York/London/Toronto

First English language edition published in 1983
by Barron's Educational Series, Inc.
© 1977 by Grafe and Unzer GmbH, Munich,
West Germany

The title of the German edition is *Kaninchen*.

All inquiries should be addressed to:
Barron's Educational Series, Inc.
113 Crossways Park Drive
Woodbury, New York 11797

International Standard Book No. 0-8120-2615-2

Inside front cover: The German Giant Checkered rabbit is one of the large breeds.

Inside back cover: Rabbits and guinea pigs can learn to get on well together.

Cover Design: Heinz Kraxenberger, Munich

Photographs

Ardea Photographics: page 64 (below right)
Bielfeld: page 28 (above right)
Coleman/Bisserot: page 54 (below left)
Coleman/Burton: page 64 (above right, above left, below left)
Coleman/Reinhard: Inside back cover
Dr. Jesse: page 53
Reinhard: Front cover, page 54 (above right), back cover (below right)
Scherz: page 28 (below)
Schmidecker: Inside front cover, pages 9, 27, 28 (above left), 54 (above left, below right), 63, back cover (below left)
Schrempp: page 10

PRINTED IN HONG KONG

3 4 5 6   041   9 8 7 6 5 4 3 2

Contents

Contents

Preface

Rabbits have become one of our favorite pets and are readily available in most pet stores. Unfortunately, we often assume that our pet is well cared for if we provide it with shelter, some dry pet food, water, and, occasionally, a carrot.

Not so!

In order for you and your children to be truly happy with your rabbit (and it with you, which is just as important), you ought to provide your pet with living conditions that best suit its nature. Only then will you, the owner, fully enjoy your pet and will it reciprocate by being cheerful, lively, and healthy.

Everything you need to know is contained in this guide. In it you will find a wealth of practical information drawn from the research of behavioral scientists, veterinarians, and dietary experts in the field of animal care.

As is true of all domestic animals, rabbits were not originally created as pets; and they retain major characteristics inherited from their ancestors in the wild. In the special section "Understanding Rabbits" you will learn some important facts about their origins and natural habitat. You will also learn how they communicate by sounds and body language. You will find out what it means, for example, when your rabbit rises up on its hind legs, beats on the floor with its hind feet, or tries to nuzzle you.

Mistakes made in acquiring and training your pet can have dire consequences because animals that are poorly handled and cared for tend to respond by biting. Turning such animals into trusting, gentle pets is extremely difficult and requires great patience as well as an intuitive ability to communicate with animals. For this reason, I have summarized in the chapter "Considerations Before You Buy" (see p. 11) everything you should keep in mind when you go to the pet store.

If you want to understand your rabbit, watch its body language. This animal is on the alert and ready to defend itself.

Rabbits are gourmets and need a varied diet. In the chapter "Correct Nutrition" (p. 34) you will find information on how to feed your rabbit and how to keep it healthy with the right diet.

Preface

Most rabbits are bought as pets for children who then have to learn how to handle the small animal gently and carefully. Your child will learn quickly, but you will have to provide firm and affectionate guidance. Our two sons, having grown up with cats and guinea pigs, have raised a dwarf rabbit in their room. Even though they both tend to be somewhat rambunctious, I have never had to interfere on behalf of their little pet. It has never suffered the least hurt, not even an accidental kick or shove. It has become second nature for my sons to protect the weak. This trait has been incorporated into their dealings with people, and I have seen this same thing happen with many children of my acquaintance. From my point of view, respect for others is a character trait which can never be taught too early in life.

The rabbits described in this guide are average animals and by no means especially selected. Any rabbit that is properly handled and cared for will turn out just as well. Our rabbit, Titus, for instance, is certainly no "super-rabbit." However, he does benefit greatly from the affection and attention he gets as well as from his almost unlimited freedom to move about. He obviously likes our family and probably thinks of us as friendly rabbit acquaintances of somewhat peculiar external appearance.

Domestic animals tend to regard humans as part of their world. It is the only way they are able to perceive us. Our human understanding enables us not to anthropomorphize animals but to treat them properly, that is, as animals. But we do need to be aware that animals are capable of experiencing pain, fear, affection, and joy. In this respect, humans and animals are similar. Oscar Heimroth, a pioneer in the study of animal behavior and the man Konrad Lorenz acknowledges as his mentor, once said, "Animals are people with a lot of emotion and very little brains." It could not be said better.

Helga Fritzsche

Do You Really Want a Rabbit?

The following questions have been formulated to aid you in deciding whether or not to buy a rabbit. They touch on your home, how much time you spend there, whether you and your family like animals, and how experienced you are with them. A genuine liking for animals means more than just being amused by them. It means the kind of affection that accepts obligations to the animal and occasional unpleasant accidents as a matter of course. Consider all the points carefully, and do not make a final decision until you have honestly answered these questions:

1. Your Home

Do you live in your own home and have a backyard?
Very good.
Do you live in an apartment with direct access to a yard?
Good.
Do you live in an apartment with a yard nearby?
Okay.
Do you live in an upstairs apartment with a fair-sized balcony?
Adequate.
Do you live in an apartment without balcony or access to a yard?
Poor.
Consider, too, that many landlords do not permit pets. Check with your landlord in advance to prevent disappointment later.

2. Time Spent at Home

Is there almost always someone at home?
Very good.
Does someone spend about half the day at home?
Adequate.
Are all family members usually gone during the day and at home just in the evening?
Very poor.

Before you decide to get a rabbit, keep in mind that it will become tame only if you spend some time with it every day.

3. Feelings towards Animals and Experience with Them

Can you imagine considering an animal part of your family? Keep in mind such things as the difficulties of planning a trip or vacation, soiled or chewed furnishings, and perhaps some nursing in case of illness—and all this over a period of about ten years. Have you ever had a pet for a considerable length of time?

Have your children ever taken care of a pet, either at home or at a friend's house? Have your children ever helped others to care for a pet?

In regard to this last question, remember that your children will learn the proper care of a pet if you are willing to teach them and if you let them assist you at first. If children are inexperienced with pets, they cannot take care of them alone.

If your answers to the questions in parts 1 and 2 are either "very good," "good," or "adequate" and those in part 3 are "yes," then by all means go ahead and buy a rabbit.

If you are gone all day, an aquarium with fish may be the only answer for you because fish do not develop a close personal relationship with people. They are satisfied with a properly tended aquarium and correct food.

If the unsuitability of your home prevents you from getting a rabbit, do not despair. There are pets that will do very well even in a high-rise apartment; for example, canaries, parakeets, finches, hamsters, and white mice. You can create proper living conditions for any of them, even without a backyard or a balcony. With proper care they will become tame and affectionate.

Considerations Before You Buy

Which Breed?

Rabbits of all breeds are suitable for life in an apartment or backyard. All rabbit strains will become tame, and most can be completely housebroken. However, dwarf rabbits are favored as pets because, with their small size, round faces, and relatively short ears, they continue to look like baby rabbits even when full grown.

Dwarf Albinos were the first dwarf rabbits. They originated from a line of wild "Polish Rabbits" that were domesticated because of their exquisitely soft fur. During the second half of the nineteenth century British breeders developed a pure white, red-eyed (albino) rabbit which produced a "substitute" ermine fur. These albinos were exhibited at shows and reintroduced to the continental market around 1900, but they did not attract too much attention. Then, however, mutations occurred in the breeder colonies: The ears became shorter; the head, broader; the body, more rotund; the whole animal, smaller. The first dwarf rabbits had been born. They attracted much interest and soon became favorites.

These small white fur bunnies remind me of alpine snow hares, but snow hares are true wild hares and cannot be crossed with pet rabbits. (Field hares and snow hares, however, can be crossbred.) Snow hares also have other characteristics in common with these albino rabbits: They are both quite social, and both dig burrows for their young.

Dwarf Albinos adapt easily to apartments and yards. They learn quickly, and even though they are very lively, they are also more "judicious" in their activities than other dwarf breeds.

Their fur is very dense, silky, and pure white. The eyes are either pale red or blue. The breed standard prescribes ears no longer than 2⅛ inches (5.5 cm.). Adults weigh between 2½ and 3½ pounds (1.25-1.75 kg.).

Like all albino animals, red-eyed rabbits are sensitive to light. The red- and blue-eyed strains also suffer more from heat because of their dense, warm coat. For that reason particular attention must be given to the temperature of the animals' environment. A shady corner is essential; temperatures should never exceed

Three particularly striking dwarf breeds: Angora, Lop, and Checkered.

11

Considerations Before You Buy

71°F (22°C); and water must always be available.

Dwarf rabbits with colored furs were introduced in 1938. A Dutch blacksmith was the first to produce this crossbreed when he mated a Dwarf Albino and a wild rabbit.

Since this breakthrough, forty years have passed, and today one can choose among many different colorings. Certain shades are officially recognized and accepted as standards for established dwarf breeds: Wild Grey, Hare Grey, Dark Grey, Iron Grey, Yellow, Black, Blue, Siamese, Madagascar, Havana, Fawn, Chinchilla, Russet, Silver, White Brindled.

All dwarf rabbits have short (up to 2¼ inches) closely set ears, a broad and relatively large head, a barely visible neck, and a short, squat body. These characteristics are all genetic remnants from the original albino line. These dwarfs, however, are not as large or heavy as their albino ancestors.

The so-called *"small" rabbits* weigh between 5 and 11 pounds (2.5-5 kg). They can easily be kept in apartments if their cages are large enough and they are frequently let out to run. Some of the small rabbit breeds are: Small Chinchilla, Siamese, Marburg Fawn, Pearl Fawn, Lux, Small Silver, English Checkered, Dutch, Tans, and Russian. The long-haired Angora rabbits

have to be combed and brushed daily. The short-haired Rex rabbits have a coat that feels like fine, silky plush.

Mixed breeds: As far as I can determine, there are as many crossbred rabbits sold in pet stores as purebreds. Crossbreeds originate from matings between different strains. They do not conform to any set standards but may be just as cute and beautifully colored as purebreds. If you do not want to breed rabbits for show, probably all that will concern you is an attractive appearance. But if you are intent on having a true dwarf strain, you will have to look for the dwarf characteristics that I described above and that are clearly evident even in very young animals. (For a list of American breeds, see Appendix.)

One, Two, or More?

If you have little spare time or are away from home even half of the day, you should not get just one animal. Rabbits need company, and they will not thrive if they are alone much of the time. This is true even though their quarters are kept clean and their diet is good.

What Rabbits Get Along Well Together?

Do not keep two male rabbits together. They may tolerate each other when they are young, but when they are full grown, they will bite and scratch so savagely that serious injuries can result.

A male and female will be troublesome and restless, and there will be frequent litters. These are not exactly ideal conditions for the average pet lover. Two animals require more care and space than a single rabbit. Also, it is not easy to find good homes for the young if you are unable to keep them yourself.

Two females will usually get along well if they were raised together or if they happen to take to each other. However, with animals that do not know each other the only way to see if they will get along is to try them together. If they do not like each other, they will fight just as males will. If they do fight, you may have to put them into separate hutches, but keep the hutches close together so that the rabbits can smell each other. That arrangement will provide them with some measure of company and mutual stimulation, and for rabbits that is far preferable to being alone.

The most desirable solution is to get two sisters from the same litter.

Male or Female?

Male and female rabbits can be completely tamed if you handle them correctly, but if they are mishandled, they will become snappy. You can

housebreak both sexes and teach them habits of cleanliness (p. 25), but both males and females may occasionally spray inside your home, especially if they do not have frequent access to a backyard or at least a balcony. They may also spray when they are excited or—in the case of males—if it is mating time.

Female   Male

Sexing young rabbits is difficult. The sexual differences are not marked yet, and it takes a trained eye to tell male from female.

Sexing Rabbits

Determining the sex of young rabbits is quite difficult. Breeders have mastered this art, but as a rule pet store owners have not. Since pet dealers order their rabbits from breeders, they will ordinarily be able

Considerations Before You Buy

to provide the sex you want. If you experience any difficulty, you may have to deal directly with a breeder (see p. 67).

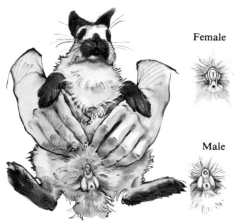

Female

Male

Sexing adults: Gentle pressure on the lower belly will make the penis protrude, but be careful not to hurt your rabbit.

Age at Time of Purchase

A young rabbit is weaned by the time it is six weeks old. The mother's milk production begins to decrease after the fourth week, and the young animals naturally come to depend more and more on an adult diet for their nourishment.

Conscientious breeders leave the young animals with their mother for at least six weeks and with their sib-lings for an additional two or three weeks.

Eight or nine weeks is the optimum age to offer rabbits for sale. Animals taken away from familiar surround-ings earlier than that are likely to die.

Where to Buy a Rabbit

Dwarf and small rabbits are usually available in most pet stores as well as in the pet sections of some depart-ment stores. However, these outlets usually do not offer much choice in breeds, and they never have a com-plete selection of colorations. If you are unable to find exactly the kind of rabbit you are looking for in the stores, you can always buy directly from a breeder. There, you can often buy a purebred animal that is being sold because, for example, its ears may be longer than standards call for, and so the animal cannot be used for breeding.

There are associations of rabbit breeders in many cities. These associations can tell you where to find certain breeds and color strains. You can find the addresses of local clubs by contacting your state rabbit breeders' association. The cost of a dwarf or small rabbit ranges from a few to several dollars, depending on breed and quality. Larger rabbit breeds are usually less expensive.

Considerations Before You Buy

Care and Housing

Before you buy your rabbit, you should decide where you want it to live. Do you want to keep it in a spacious, sturdy rabbit hutch outside, in a sufficiently roomy cage inside (with a daily romp in one of your rooms or on your balcony), or will you give it the free run of your house or apartment?

Once you have decided this general question, you can then determine the best specific location in your house or yard. Also, you will be spared buying supplies that may later be unnecessary.

The Right Place for the Hutch or Cage

These points should now be carefully considered:

• The cage must be easily accessible for cleaning and feeding at all times.
• Rabbits cannot tolerate heat. Avoid placing the cage next to a radiator or in a spot exposed to the hot noon or afternoon sun.
• Rabbits do not tolerate drafts. Check the selected spot for drafts when you are airing out your room. Always raise the cage away from the floor, where it is often too cold and drafty.
• Be sure that the cage shuts securely so that the rabbit cannot get out and fall to the floor.
• The cage has to be secured in place to prevent it from being accidentally tipped over.
• Do not keep your rabbit in the same room with the television. High frequencies inaudible for us are painful for animals. Also, a family room is often too noisy even when the television is off.
• Rabbits do not tolerate moisture, and an outdoor hutch has to be protected from rain and wind and from snow during the winter. You will need to weatherproof the shelter with tar paper. The open side of the hutch should have a southeast or south exposure, not one to the north or west.

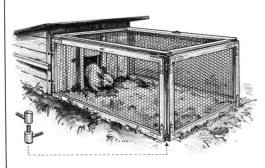

This hutch with an attached run that can be taken apart provides your rabbit with good weatherproof housing.

15

Considerations Before You Buy

• Even outdoor rabbit hutches should be raised somewhat above the ground (2–3 ft.). The doors should close securely and be provided with a lock. If you are fortunate enough to have a well-ventilated shed, that is an ideal place for a hutch.

The Right Place for the Run

Try to place the rabbit's run so that it is protected from strong winds and offers some shade at all times. Remember that the sun moves during the course of the day! Rabbits often die of heatstroke if they are unable to find a shady corner in hot weather.

If your rabbit will be left unattended outdoors for several hours, make sure that the run offers some protection from rain (see illustration on page 15).

Remember also that placing the run on a lawn or a meadow will give enterprising animals the chance to dig their way out of the run, and it is therefore essential to check on your charge from time to time.

If you do not have a backyard, the run can be put on a porch, a balcony, or even in one of your rooms. The available space will, of course, dictate the size and nature of the run.

Free Run of a Balcony

Your rabbit can live quite happily on a balcony if provided with a

weatherproof hutch (see illustrations on pages 19–20). If you let your rabbit have the run of your balcony during the day, place a carpet remnant or doormat covered with a piece of blanket in a well-protected corner. The animal needs a warm nesting place of this kind because the concrete floor of the balcony is often cold. Remember to add a litter box (p. 21) and perhaps a scratch box as well. When the door to your balcony is open but you want your animal to remain outside, you can block the door with a frame about 2 to 3 feet high and covered with wire netting or chicken wire (see drawing below).

Your rabbit will signal that it wants to come in by sitting up on its hind legs.

16

Considerations Before You Buy

Many balcony railings have gaps in them large enough for dwarf rabbits to squeeze through. You can prevent your rabbit from falling off such a balcony by placing three-foot chicken wire around the balcony and securing it tightly to the railing. Three feet is not excessively high: Our rabbit Titus can easily jump 2½ feet without a running start. If your rabbit has the run of your house, balcony, and yard (as ours does), you will need a draft-free place for its sleeping box. You will also need a special location for the litter box, especially if your pet cannot run free outside every day or when the weather prevents you from taking it outside at least three times a day. The feeding dish and water bowl should be located where they are not in the way but where your pet can always get at them.

What to Look for When Buying a Rabbit

Most rabbits offered for sale by stores or breeders are healthy, but you should be able to recognize symptoms indicating possible health problems. Obviously, you do not want to buy a sick animal that may not live long after your purchase.

Checklist for Signs of Health and Disease

The *eyes* should neither be watery nor show signs of any other kind of discharge.

The *nose* is usually dry in healthy animals, and a pink color of the mucous membranes indicates good circulation. The nostrils move evenly in respiration, revealing the mucous membrane. On an especially hot day, the nostrils move more rapidly even in healthy animals. Unusually rapid breathing and a bluish discoloration of the mucous membranes (especially visible in light-skinned animals) are symptoms of heart and lung problems or may indicate circulatory weakness as a result of an infection. Frequent sneezing may indicate snuffles, a dangerous and highly contagious disease.

The *ears* of a healthy rabbit are sensitive to all sounds, even very soft ones. The interior of the ears should be perfectly clean. Even a slight deposit or scab may be a sign of ear mite infestation, which can be fatal if left untreated.

The *teeth* should not be too long or bent into horn-like or circular shapes. These deformities indicate improper positioning of the teeth, and animals so affected cannot eat solid foods and do not develop well. It is useless to clip such teeth. This causes the

Considerations Before You Buy

animal severe pain and is only of temporary value because a rabbit's teeth keep growing.

A healthy animal has a shiny *coat*, and the fur is smooth in short-haired breeds. Dull, shaggy, or rough fur is a sign of poor health. Fur standing on end in a cold room may simply mean that the animal is cold. However, if the temperature is normal, this sign is symptomatic of illness. Bald spots on the ears, head, or back may be due to a lack of certain vitamins or to mange mite infestation. You will not be able to determine the cause of this abnormality; and, therefore, you should not buy an animal with it.

The *belly* should be somewhat round and the overall shape slightly plump. However, a belly that is unusually large, bloated, and perhaps even hard to the touch (unless you are dealing with a pregnant doe) is a sign of a serious disorder.

Fecal matter stuck around the *anus* and on the belly indicates poor digestion and possible diarrhea due to premature weaning. This problem can also arise with animals that have been properly weaned but have been exposed to cold and drafts or have had an incorrect diet.

Injuries from bites are often found on males that have been kept together too long after reaching sexual maturity. Biting may also occur between female rabbits unfamiliar with each other. These injuries can easily be spotted on the legs and head. By gently stroking against the natural growth of the fur, you can detect bites on the body, especially on the back and sides. With appropriate treatment these wounds will heal well. If you want to be safe, however, consult your veterinarian.

Small scratches heal by themselves. Animals with an even disposition respond well to careful, gentle petting and do not show anger or react by biting. This is especially true of young animals and also of older animals that have always been well treated. Some rabbits show their pleasure by gently pressing their bodies against your hand when you pet them. Never thump your rabbit the way you would a dog, and never run your fingers against the natural growth of the fur.

Housing and Equipment

Rabbit Cages for Indoors

Many different types of rabbit cages are available in pet and department stores. The U.S. Federal Animal Welfare Act requires that a cage for a large adult rabbit be at least 14 inches high and have a floor area of 4 square feet or more. Minimum requirements for various rabbit weights are:

Up to 4 pounds:	1.5 sq. ft.
4 to 8 pounds:	3 sq. ft.
8 to 12 pounds:	4 sq. ft.
Over 12 pounds:	5 sq. ft.

In all cases, minimum height is 14 inches.

The floor can be a plastic pan, or it can be a grate over a pan that collects the excreta. Choose a material that is easy to clean and a design that is handy. The type of bedding you use

A plastic cage can easily get too hot. Never place a cage like this in direct sunlight.

will determine the depth of the pan. If the litter box will be in the cage, the sides of the litter box should be high enough to prevent the rabbit from scratching the litter out of the box.

This is a better indoor cage than the enclosed plastic type. This cage should be kept out of drafts.

A transparent plastic hood with a grate for ventilation can be useful, but the plastic hood diminishes air flow and raises the temperature. A cage with wire grating for sides may therefore be preferable. A hay feeder should be included with any cage.

Rabbit Hutches for Balcony, Terrace, or Yard

Homemade rabbit hutches are just as good as commercial ones, and they present no major problems for the home builder. Plywood is a good material, but it should be treated or painted to be made water-resistant.

19

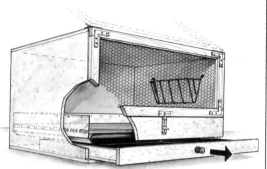

If you want to build your own cage, this is a practical design with a removable tray for cleaning.

The door consists of a wooden frame covered with wire mesh. You can buy wire mesh commonly used for rabbit cages, but hardware cloth with openings not much larger than ¼ " is better.

To prevent the floor from soaking up urine, tar the surface, then cover it with another board that can be replaced from time to time. Instead of using a board, you can cover the floor with a waterproof material like Formica or use a plastic pan that covers the whole floor.

This type of housing can be used indoors as well as outdoors.

The Homemade Run

If you cannot let your rabbit run free indoors or outdoors, you will need a run or a fenced-in area. The frame of this run can be built from two-by-fours with diagonals to strengthen it. The sides and top are then covered with chicken wire. It is essential to cover the top to prevent dogs, cats, or wild animals from getting at the rabbits.

A run for fair-weather use. Remember to provide a shaded area in this type of run.

A child's playpen covered with chicken wire can serve quite nicely as a rabbit run. If the run has to be placed on a balcony, on a terrace, or in a room, you will have to put it on an impervious surface, such as painted plywood or Formica. Layers of newspapers can be placed in one corner as litter. These are easy to change, but some rabbits will scatter them. If the run is large enough, the litter box can be put inside it.

The rabbit also needs something soft and warm to sleep on. An old baby blanket or towel is more practical than straw or hay.

The Litter Box

Rabbits do not like to go to the bathroom where they sleep. They prefer a litter box and will use their sleeping area only if they have no choice. A friend of mine has a rabbit that goes to the bathroom in the guinea pig's box, thus keeping his own living quarters clean.

You will need a plastic pan that is not too shallow. A cat box that you can purchase in any pet store is ideal. Some pet stores have a particularly practical model with a detachable top frame that prevents the litter from spilling over the sides.

Bedding

Sand, peat, moss, and sawdust are not suitable beddings for indoor cages. Sawdust is not good for outdoor caging either because it spoils the rabbit's coat. The best choice is cat litter. That type of mineral litter is not only absorbent but also odorless and dust free.

Rabbit hutches built to stand in a garage, stable, or backyard can use a layer of peat moss covered with straw, hay, or dry leaves as bedding. (A tip for gardeners: Put your used rabbit bedding on your compost heap to produce excellent humus.) The sleeping box or quarter can be lined with newspaper, which is easily changed when soiled. Although it is a good idea to check the box daily, you need not change the papers every day. For a rabbit that runs free, a thick layer of hay or straw on top of newspaper can serve nicely as resting quarters, too.

Gravel or Sandbox for Scratching

Some rabbits like to scratch actively in their litter box if they have little access to the outdoors. For that reason, the box should have high sides. Cat litter boxes are fine, but if you have an indoor rabbit that is particularly given to scratching, you may want a box with gravel or sand in it. Fine gravel is better than sand because sand sticks to the hair. Clean garden dirt is best of all.

Food and Water Dishes

A heavy earthenware bowl is best for dry food. If you feed other foods, such as greens, inside the cage, too, you should have a second bowl for them so that they will not be soiled with feces and urine.

Housing and Equipment

Do not use any lightweight bowls that tip easily. Plastic dishes are dangerous because rabbits nibble on them and inadvertently swallow sharp fragments of plastic. Earthenware bowls cost between $2 and $5.

The glass or ceramic food bowl (above) should have a broad base. Regular narrow-based bowls (below) spill easily and are not suitable.

For rabbits that run free, drinking water can be offered in another heavy bowl. In indoor cages and runs bottles with sipper tubes are more practical.

If your rabbits are kept outdoors you need to supply water only for pregnant or nursing does, provided there are enough fresh greens available. Additional water is also necessary in the heat of the summer. Suspended bottles with sipper tubes cost between $2 and $4.

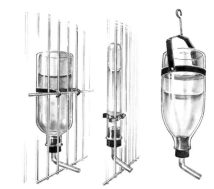

Water in the cage or hutch is best supplied in bottles with sipper tubes. Three commercially available models are illustrated here.

I recommend that you buy some dry food pellets from the breeder or pet store where you purchase your rabbit. Make sure it is the same type of food your rabbit has been eating until then. If you do not have a cheaper source of hay, buy some from the dealer or breeder, too.

Leashes

A rabbit leash comes in handy on trips or during bad weather when you have to take your rabbit out for a walk. You will need a very small dog harness with an attachable leash. The leash will be too short and can be lengthened to at least 5 feet by tying some cord to it. Harness and leash cost between $5 and $12.

Basic Rules for Care

Taking Your Pet Home and Making It Feel at Home

First of all, the shortest route home is the best one. Avoid all detours on the trip to your pet's new home. In "Car or Train Travel" (p. 47) you will find detailed information about various carriers and containers for transporting the animal, as well as how to make him as comfortable as possible while traveling. By the time your rabbit arrives at your home, he will have endured quite a lot of excitement and some anxious moments: removal from a familiar cage; separation from siblings; strange voices and scents; and, last but not least, the trip itself.

The new environment may have quite an unsettling effect at first, too. Put your rabbit into his new, fully equipped cage. Pet your rabbit gently, and then give him time to sniff and smell and examine his new quarters. Once he realizes there is no danger, he will quickly accept them as his refuge and home.

When you see your rabbit take a drink, eat, and groom himself, you can consider the initiation period over. Your pet is beginning to feel comfortable and at home.

Do not forget to pet the new family member often and hold him on your lap where he can snuggle up to you the way rabbits do among themselves. Rabbits need frequent physical contact, and they become withdrawn if they are left alone too much.

This is especially true for young animals that have just been weaned and separated from their siblings. Be sure that your rabbit has frequent opportunities during his initial days with you to smell all members of your family and as many objects as possible in his new environment. Allow plenty of time, and leave him alone while he familiarizes himself this way with everything that is new to him.

Remember to keep him away from all electrical cords and wiring he could gnaw on. This could prove fatal for the animal and very unpleasant for you (see "Preventing Accidents," p. 32). Also, keep books and sheet music out of his reach.

Acquainting Your Rabbit with Other Pets

Here are some suggestions on helping your rabbit adjust to other pets in your household:
• Avoid the temptation to neglect other pets because of the newcomer. Pay enough attention to them so that no jealousy toward the newcomer arises.
• Allow time for your rabbit to feel safe and at home before permitting

Basic Rules for Care

other pets to approach him. Even then, leave him in his closed hutch at their first meeting.

• Allow your dog, cat, and rabbit plenty of time to sniff and smell each other. Speak quietly to all of them, and pet each one of them in turn. If your dog barks or tries to jump or paw at the rabbit's cage, respond with a firm, loud "No!" Cats too may want to paw at the newcomer and should be disciplined in the same manner.

• You have to be absolutely certain that your rabbit is safe and that nothing will happen to him before you give your dog, cat, and rabbit the free run of your home without supervision. Once your rabbit has been badly frightened, the only responses he may be capable of are fear and flight; these responses are the very ones that will provoke other animals to pursuit. Our Titus is without fear when it comes to cats. Fortunately, his first encounter with a cat was with our old Beppi, who was always friendly with him. He seems to consider cats his peers, and whenever our neighbor's tomcat or our kitten Putti gets too rambunctious or too rough with him, our rabbit successfully defends himself with punching, biting, or special jumps designed to impress his adversaries.

• Remember that misunderstandings among animals of different types are common because of differences in their "languages." Cats, for example, tend to interpret the provocative, aggressive jumps of a buck rabbit as acceptance of their own fondness for play and chasing. Rabbits, however, are usually cautious and gentle in their dealings with their "friends" and will probably misunderstand the playfulness of cats and dogs as aggression by a member of their peer group or as an attack by a predator.

I know from experience that not all dogs can learn to live harmoniously with a rabbit because they are unable to stop seeing it as potential prey. This is especially true if the dog is no longer a puppy and you let your rabbit run at large.

It is easier to train cats to get along with rabbits, provided you are dealing with well-fed, thoroughly domesticated cats.

Guinea pigs often get along surprisingly well with rabbits but not always. And if there are differences, the guinea pig is the loser because he is not as nimble as the rabbit and may sustain bites from him.

Our first rabbit, Caesar, was in the habit of licking our guinea pig Squirrel behind the ears. At first we thought this was cute. But when the guinea pig's squealing prompted us to check more closely, we found a bald,

Basic Rules for Care

bleeding spot. This suggested something other than affection, and from then on, we kept the two animals apart.

In the section "What Rabbits Get Along Well Together?" (p. 12) I offer suggestions for keeping two rabbits together.

Grooming and Housebreaking

Rabbits are among the cleanest animals there are. They spend more time grooming themselves than cats do, and that is saying a lot. So, please, never give your rabbit a bath. It is a good idea to brush your pet daily during the shedding seasons (spring and fall) because brushing stimulates the circulation and helps the animal put this somewhat strenuous period quickly behind him.

Rabbits always relieve themselves

in the same place in their hutch. In this inborn behavior they follow the example of their relatives in the wild that establish special "bathrooms" in their dens and burrows.

This litter box has a rim that lets the rabbit scratch without throwing the litter out of the box.

Housebreaking your rabbit, then, should be limited to getting him used to one particular spot from the first day you have him home. If you leave the choice up to him, he may choose a corner under your bed or behind a sofa, neither of which locations is likely to please you.

It is therefore important to have his litter box available for him before you allow him his first free run in your home. Put him into the box right away, and he may well make proper use of it the first time he scratches and sniffs in the litter. Because he engages in this activity

Grooming tools. Brushing and combing are essential every day during shedding.

25

with much gusto, make sure the sides of your litter box are at least 4 inches high. On page 21 I described a litter box with an additional elevated top frame that has an overall height of 6 inches.

Some soap and warm water are all that is needed if your rabbit should urinate on your floor or carpet. Because your animal will want to continue using this particular spot in the future, you would do well to cover it for a few days, the obvious and most appropriate cover being the litter box. Never use newspaper or rags to cover the spot because your pet can easily move them and uncover the desired area.

It is entirely normal for the rabbit to drop a few bean-like feces when he is excited. They are dry and can easily be swept up without leaving any trace.

There is no point in scolding or punishing the animal. Indeed, if you make the animal anxious and aggressive it may never become housebroken. Only attention, patience, and gentleness will produce the desired results.

If the animal has to spend much of the day in his cage, clean at least the "bathroom corner" every day. It takes just a few minutes; the animal will be comfortable; and your home will be free of odors.

If your rabbit has the free run of your home, check the litter box daily. Your pet will avoid the box and find a new spot if the litter box is wet and soiled.

Some friends of ours came up with an ingenious and inexpensive arrangement for the litter box: they place a sheet of newspaper on the bottom of the litter box and cover it with cat litter. The box is emptied daily, and only the wet litter sticks to the newspaper. The paper and wet litter are thrown out; the bottom of the box is covered with clean newspaper; and the remaining dry litter is put back in the box. The dry fecal matter in the litter can remain there. With this method you need to change all the litter only once a week.

If your home is a downstairs apartment and opens onto a yard as ours does, there is still another possibility to consider. Our rabbit Titus is accustomed to relieving himself outside, if at all possible. If he wants to go out, he will either stand on his hind legs or scratch and paw at the carpet. Weather permitting, we let him run outdoors on his own. During rainy weather and before retiring in the evening, we take him out on his leash. He likes certain spots, and we let him scratch and sniff in them for a while. The whole procedure takes only five or ten minutes, and he is

then usually able to wait until morning before he has to go again. Our neighbors find it amusing to see us take our "dog" for a walk.

Using a Leash

Dwarf rabbits can be trained to a leash and harness at about 2½–3 months.

Harness and leash (available in pet and department stores) for walking your rabbit.

Get another family member to help you if you are dealing with an animal that is unusually lively and fidgety or if you feel unsure of yourself in dealing with rabbits. One of you can hold the rabbit and pet him while the other puts the harness on him and fastens it securely. But be sure that the harness is not closed too tightly, or it may hurt the animal. Now pick him up, and carry him to where you want him to run.

At this point, you may have to revise your thinking. Unlike a dog, which learns to walk on a leash with a minimum of patience on your part, a rabbit is quite different. A dog learns easily because he basically respects his master as his superior and leader. Although there is a kind of "pecking order" among rabbits, they do not recognize any leaders, and this is why you cannot take a rabbit for a walk the way you can a dog.

Let your rabbit sniff, dig, and hop around as he likes. Let him lead you. Simply stand still and hold the leash firmly if there are certain places your rabbit should not explore, such as a street or a flower bed. Or you can pick him up and carry him to a location that is not off limits. Allow him to move around in this way for at least a quarter of an hour.

Of course, a rabbit prefers to run free outdoors without harness or leash. But at night, in cold and rainy weather, in an unfamiliar environment, or on trips, this simply is not possible. In such cases, you will have to walk your rabbit on a leash.

Small and Large Runs

The ideal solution for a rabbit is to have the run of the entire home. In our house, only the living room remains closed to Titus during the day.

29

Basic Rules for Care

In the evening, he joins the family even there. Most of the time he rests quietly and is content to be petted because he was allowed to run free during the day. If he starts to gnaw on something, we can easily distract him by petting him. However, when he was still very young and had a strong urge to gnaw, we were sometimes forced to remove him from the living room.

Once your rabbit is familiar with the inside of your home he can begin to explore the balcony, his run, or your fenced yard. At first, you ought to watch him or at least check on him frequently.

Our Titus has the free run of our entire yard during the winter months (October to March). During the summer, he is allowed only in our fenced frontyard where the shrubbery is not as susceptible to harm. If he digs some holes, we just fill them in again. He obviously prefers to have the run of both front and backyard, but in the summer he does too much damage in the backyard. And there is plenty of room for him in the front.

But there are other solutions. Friends of ours have an apartment with a balcony but no yard or nearby place where their pet rabbit can run loose. While this is not the best possible setup, these friends give their rabbit the run of their entire apartment.

They have decided to accept him as a member of the family. No one is upset by occasional gnawings. Droppings and small puddles cause no alarm and are quickly cleaned up.

The rabbit responds to this gentle and understanding treatment by being lively, cheerful, and affectionate. It is so trusting that it will even jump into visitors' laps.

Points to Remember When Handling Rabbits

• Avoid loud noise and hectic behavior, particularly at first when your new pet is nervous and easily frightened.
• Leave it alone when it wants peace and quiet (see ''Body Language,'' p. 55). Even children will develop this kind of consideration if you teach it to them with firmness, kindness, and consistency and set a good example for them.

Although petting and stroking the animal are important, they are not always desirable. No creature likes to be bothered when eating or sleeping, for example.
• Pick up your rabbit as you would your cat. If you feel uncertain and are not used to handling animals, pick the rabbit up by the loose fur between the shoulder blades. Take a

Basic Rules for Care

firm hold, but do not be rough. Bring your other arm close to your body and place the small rabbit on your lower arm. Support its rump with your hand; its front paws should rest in the bend of your elbow (see drawings).

• Very small children should not pick up the rabbit. If handled improperly, it may kick or scratch, it can hurt the child, or it may fall and suffer serious injury (such as a broken leg). Older children have to be carefully taught how to pick up a rabbit, and you should continue to supervise them until they know how to do it properly.

Young children also have to be taught to be gentle and to pet a rabbit the "right way," that is, in the direction of the growth of fur. Never let your children grab an animal by its ears or its tail!

Children will learn faster if you let them help take care of your rabbit. You can start to assign small tasks to them as soon as you feel that they have the necessary understanding of the animal and can assume responsibility for its care. But even children who love animals and are careful with them sometimes forget their duties when other more exciting things come up. The main responsibility of caretaking will therefore be yours. Whether you choose to remind your

To pick up a rabbit take it by the scruff of the neck with one hand and

place it on your other forearm, supporting its hind quarters with your hand.

31

children or whether you decide to take care of the rabbit yourself from time to time the animal needs regular and daily care.

• Rough handling is not the only thing that will make rabbits nervous and snappy. Teasing and taunting the animal "for fun" have the same effect.

• Your rabbit needs not only the necessities, such as food, cleanliness, and regular exercise, but also daily contact with its "family." Talk softly to your rabbit. Pet its head and back, its silky cheeks, the bridge of the nose all the way to the forehead. If you thump your rabbit's sides or rumple its fur as you would with a dog, the rabbit will feel attacked and may respond by growling and biting.

Preventing Accidents

• Open and shut all doors carefully, and use a doorstop if you want a door to stay open. A sudden draft could slam the door shut, and your rabbit might be caught.

• Stepping on the animal by accident can cause fractures and paralysis. Be especially careful if the rabbit runs around loose in your home.

• Electrical cords and wiring can be fatal because rabbits love to gnaw and chew on just about anything. Disconnect cords and place them out

Back injuries can result from stepping on a rabbit or catching it accidentally in a door. These injuries can lead to paralysis.

of the animal's reach if it has to be left alone for a few hours or a whole day.

• Telephone cords are less hazardous, but it is a good idea to keep them away from your rabbit. If you do not, you may be in for a surprise. Friends of ours once found a cord chewed in half when they needed to make an urgent phone call.

• Cars and dogs are always a danger to your rabbit. Be sure you have shut the gate to your yard if your rabbit is loose in it. If you take him outdoors to a meadow or wooded area, keep him on his leash so that you can pick him up quickly if danger threatens.

• Closed runs should always be covered on top. Here the rabbit has no chance to escape if it should be attacked from above by stray dogs or cats, weasels, hawks, or owls.

Basic Rules for Care

• A fall from your arms, a cage, or a balcony can be potentially fatal. Make sure you pick up your rabbit properly (p. 30). See that cage, hutch, and house doors latch securely (p. 15), and cover your balcony railing with wire mesh (p. 17).

• At night a rabbit should be kept inside your home or in a sturdy, safe rabbit hutch.

This is the right way to hold your rabbit. Remember, though, that he can injure himself with a sudden jump out of your arms.

• Heat and moisture are unhealthy for rabbits. Whether you keep your rabbit on a balcony, in a run, or in a yard, always remember to protect him from rain and have a shady corner available. When you take him on a trip in your car, never place his cage over the car's engine; and never leave your rabbit in a parked car on a warm day.

Correct Nutrition

Basic Rules: All feed must be fresh, not too cold, and not drenched with dew or rain. Always remove the uneaten food from the previous day. If you use commercially prepared foods, check the expiration date on the package. Do not feed your rabbit food straight out of the refrigerator. Let the food reach room temperature. Shake greens to remove excess moisture, and feed them only in small portions, preferably mixed with chopped hay or straw.

Do not let greens get mixed into the bedding. When the rabbit lies down on them, they will get warm, rot, get mixed with urine and feces, and possibly cause serious intestinal problems.

Hay should be stored in a dry, well-aired place. If it becomes moist or moldy, it can produce fatal intestinal disorders. Anything that grows in or near areas treated with herbicides or pesticides or within 500 yards of highways or freeways should be considered dangerous.

Sweets of any kind are forbidden even if your rabbit likes them.

Rabbits that spend most of their time in a cage or hutch should be fed only once or twice a day, morning and afternoon. Because they get little exercise they will get overweight if fed more often (see Feeding Chart, page 38). Rabbits that get a lot of exercise

can be fed more generously. They eat only from need, not from boredom, as caged rabbits will. Exercise keeps them in good shape. You can leave dry pellets, greens, hay, and water in front of these active rabbits at all times.

In the spring and fall when the rabbits are shedding, their food should be especially rich in proteins and vitamins: a wide variety of greens, good hay, rolled oats, and pellets.

Any change in diet should be made slowly and carefully: e.g., a change from pellets to mixed fresh foods soon after you have purchased your rabbit or a change to varied greens in the spring. Too rapid a change would be dangerous for the rabbit's health. Always start out with the same food the rabbit was receiving in its original home, then introduce new foods slowly after the animal is acclimatized.

Food bowls must be kept meticulously clean at all times.

Where food is concerned, rabbits are individualists. One rabbit may crave what another rejects, and you may have to try a number of feeds to find what appeals to your rabbit.

Rabbits' teeth never stop growing. While still in the womb, rabbits start grinding their teeth to prevent them from growing into their jaws. Later

Correct Nutrition

in life, they need crunchy foods every day to keep their teeth short and healthy.

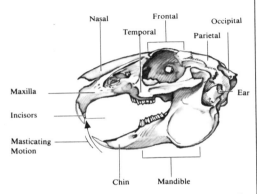

Anatomy of a rabbit skull. Because a rabbit's teeth never stop growing, tough, crunchy foods are essential to keep the teeth worn down.

What Rabbits Should Eat

Rabbits should get hay, pellets, and fresh greens every day.

Dry Feeds
Rabbit pellets (e.g., Purina or Wayne Rabbit Chow) are available in pet stores and feed stores. You should request food designed for breeder animals because most manufacturers also produce foods designed to fatten meat rabbits.

Pellets in small packages are more expensive but are useful in determining your rabbit's preferences.

Many rabbits prefer thick rolled oats, which are nourishing and easily digestible. If you feed whole oats, the rabbits will leave the hulls. Table oatmeal is not good because there is nothing left for the rabbit to chew.

Hay
Hay is mandatory because it keeps the digestive tract healthy. Good quality hay consists of a variety of grasses, dandelion, clover, etc. Wild flowers enrich hay quality and enhance the flavor. If you cut your own hay, you should cut it during warm weather and dry it as quickly as possible. That will prevent the loss of valuable nutrients. If you have to buy hay, you will do well to get it from a farmer or feed store. Hay from second cuttings is good for baby rabbits and weak animals because it is tender. Alfalfa is the best hay you can buy. It is sold loose or pressed into small cubes that are easy to feed and prevent waste.

Supplementary Foods
The following can be added in small amounts: whole oats, cracked corn, dried whole wheat bread.

Greens and Other Fresh Foods
Greens should always be fed in a mix of various grasses and greens; avoid feeding just one kind of green.

Correct Nutrition

If you have a large enough yard, you can seed different grasses and let your rabbit graze on them. You can harvest as hay whatever the rabbit has not eaten. Grass seeds are available in nurseries and feed stores.

Fresh foods that you can either grow in your garden or buy at the store (Be sure to wash all produce that you buy!) are: carrots and carrot tops, endive, chicory, radish greens, kohlrabi with its leaves, turnips with leaves, cauliflower stem and leaves, Chinese cabbage, Brussel sprouts, Jerusalem artichokes, kale, fresh corn, soybean and pea greens (not the beans and pods!). Herbs are good also: sage, mint, parsley, young mustard greens, camomile. You can also feed pieces of apple, apple parings, and raw potatoes.

Fresh foods in the winter months: Apples, potatoes, endive, chicory, Chinese cabbage, Brussel sprouts, cauliflower—all are available in stores. Sprouts can be grown in your kitchen; carrots can be kept in a cool cellar; some hardy greens can even be wintered over in your garden. Remember to let all cold, fresh greens warm to room temperature before feeding.

Greens you can gather on a walk: dandelion greens, shepherd's purse, cow-parsnip, and young nettles.

Branches to nibble on: leafy branches from beeches, maples, willows, hazelnuts, and fruit trees.

Plants known to bloat and cause diarrhea: green, red, and Savoy cabbage, iceberg lettuce, red clover, and feed turnips. These should be fed sparingly and preferably mixed with other greens.

Poisonous Plants

Poisoning of rabbits by plants has hardly ever been reported. Wooly pod or broad-leafed milkweed (Pacific Southwest) is known to be poisonous. Ladino clover causes infertility; comfrey, dock, buttercup, and wild parsnip have been implicated as toxic. Oleander is poisonous for people and—we assume—for rabbits.

Wild rabbits and hares avoid poisonous plants, but domestic rabbits have lost the capacity to differentiate.

Water

Rabbits that live indoors should always have access to fresh water that is not too cold. Rabbits that live outdoors and have constant access to greens need water only on hot days.

One large carrot (about 3 oz.) provides enough water for one whole day for a dwarf rabbit. This method of *water substitution* is used primarily for rabbits that are kept outdoors in rabbit hutches.

Correct Nutrition

A *salt lick* is recommended for rabbits that are kept indoors continually and have constant access to water. Suspend the lick at a comfortable height in the cage where the rabbit can reach it easily.

Details about the nutrition of pregnant and nursing does are given in the chapter "Rabbit Breeding and Production" (page 48).

Since every rabbit has particular likes and dislikes, you should take the following feeding chart as a guide only, not as a set of fixed feeding rules.

Young rabbits quickly learn to drink from a sipper tube.

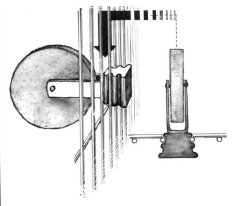

A salt lick can prevent mineral deficiencies. It can be fastened to the side of the cage with a bracket.

Correct Nutrition

Feeding Chart

Caged Rabbits with a limited exercise area should have daily rations of this type:

Summer

Mornings:	1 oz. (1 handful) pellets or thick rolled oats.
Afternoons:	3–5½ oz. (2 handfuls) mixed greens plus a piece of carrot, potato, or turnip. Every other day, 1 piece of hard bread or 1 tablespoon whole oats; and branches to nibble.

Winter

Mornings:	1 oz. (1 handful) pellets or thick rolled oats.
Afternoons:	1 large carrot (about 3 oz.); also, alternately, apples and greens; every other day, 1 piece of hard bread or 1 tablespoon of whole oats; and branches to nibble.

Hay should always be available.

Rabbits Free to Run Indoors or Outdoors should have daily rations of this type:

Summer and Winter

Mornings:	Dry pellets or thick rolled oats in unlimited quantities.
All day:	Fresh water available at all times; daily fresh mixed greens. If rabbits are free to run outdoors for several hours each day, they find enough to nibble on and do not need additional greens or nibbles.

Young Animals should be fed pellets and hay. Any greens have to be of the most easily digestible types. Absolutely none of the bloating greens can be fed, not even in the smallest quantities (see page 36). The young rabbit develops intestinal flora (useful bacteria that aid in the breakdown and digestion of foods) only slowly. Intestinal problems due to improper nutrition occur most frequently and are most dangerous in rabbits under six months of age.

When Your Rabbit Is Sick

A rabbit that was healthy when purchased and that has been well cared for will not tend to get sick. It has enough resistance to fight off most bacteria and viruses before a disease can take hold.

Prevention, however, is the best medicine—for rabbits as well as for people. That is why I have given so much attention to proper maintenance and care: a clean, roomy hutch in an appropriate location; good nutrition; daily exercise (indoors or out); regular grooming, especially during shedding; adequate rest; friendly interaction; and an awareness that rabbits have to live in harmony with their rabbit nature (see "Understanding Rabbits," page 52).

There are times, however, when rabbits are more susceptible to disease: does during pregnancy and nursing cycles; Angora rabbits right after shearing; all rabbits during shedding and extreme weather conditions. If you know your rabbit well and provide extra care at the appropriate times (keeping the Angoras warm after shearing, for example) you will probably have no problems at all.

Hutches and cages should be thoroughly cleaned and disinfected every three months. Pet stores offer a variety of safe and suitable detergents and disinfectants.

It is important that you observe this rule: New rabbits and ones you already have should be kept apart for at least 2–3 weeks. Feed your new animals and clean their cages separately; then wash your hands carefully. Remember that you, too, can become a carrier of disease.

Be sure to keep plastics away from your rabbits. Even soft plastic is dangerous because it becomes hard and sharp in the stomach and intestines.

In the "Checklist for Signs of Health and Disease" (page 17) I mentioned some indicators of general ill health. In this section I will describe the specific symptoms of common diseases as well as of some rarer but more serious ones.

Diarrhea is the most frequent cause of death in young rabbits. This disease may sometimes be caused by an abrupt change from dry food to green. Moldy hay or other spoiled, wet, or unsuitable feeds can be the cause, as can cold drafts or moist bedding. Chemicals such as weed killers or pesticides on feed can be the culprit.

Symptoms: The fecal matter is soft or runny, has a bad odor, maybe a bit sour, and sometimes shows some blood.

Treatment: Change bedding once or twice per day. Clean food containers daily with hot water and detergent. Stop feeding greens. The most suitable feed is good hay, preferably alfalfa. You may want to boil rice lightly, dry it, and feed that. As liquids you can offer water, camomile or mint tea, or very thin black tea. If diarrhea persists, you should see a veterinarian. A disease may be causing the diarrhea, and prolonged diarrhea weakens rabbits quickly.

Constipation can develop from an abrupt change from greens to dry feed. Nursing does are more susceptible when they are not offered sufficient water; fever or infectious diseases can also be the cause.

Symptoms: There is either little or no fecal matter in the cage. Animals may sit listlessly in a corner with humped-up backs and refuse to eat. Occasionally, the belly may appear bloated.

Treatment: Offer lots of water at room temperature, juicy carrots, endive, or apple parings. Wash all produce carefully to get rid of chemicals. Allow as much space and exercise as possible. Medication should be given only if a specific disease agent is evident.

Bloating is an intestinal problem that involves the overproduction and accumulation of gas. Possible causes are red clover, cabbage (too much of it), wet food, cold food, and food fermented by excessively warm storage. As mentioned before, young animals are the most susceptible because their intestinal flora are not yet fully established. Also susceptible are animals that are weak for some reason, as after a bout with disease. Bloating can be fatal.

Symptoms: The abdomen is greatly distended and often hard to the touch. The gas-filled intestine causes much pressure and may give rise to shortness of breath and cardiovascular weakness. The lack of oxygen is evidenced in a pale bluish discoloration of ears and lips.

Treatment: Sudden and extreme bloating is usually fatal. When you see the first indication of bloating, immediately remove all food and take away all edible bedding. To empty the intestinal tract quickly, feed the rabbit a teaspoonful of linseed oil. Do not drop the oil on food. You must give it directly. Hold the rabbit still, and have a helper empty the teaspoon of oil carefully into the side of the mouth in the pocket between the lips and teeth. Wait until the rabbit has swallowed before you let it go. If you cannot manage to restrain the animal and administer the medicine, get help from a veterinarian.

To offset circulatory weakness, you can feed a spoonful of strong coffee.

When Your Rabbit Is Sick

Coccidiosis is a parasitic disease. It is caused by one-celled organisms that can severely damage the intestinal lining. These organisms spend part of their life cycle in the rabbit's intestines and part in bedding and food. Thus, the more often you clean the bedding, the less the chance of infection is.

Symptoms: By the time symptoms appear, the infection is at an advanced stage. Diarrhea, sometimes with blood, is the most frequent sign of heavy infestation. Sometimes bloating can occur if the food is no longer being adequately digested. The more advanced the disease, the more likely it will be fatal. Naturally, young and weakened animals will be the first to succumb.

To be sure of the diagnosis, you have to take a stool sample to a veterinarian.

Treatment: The veterinarian has several effective medications available. However, a diagnosis has to be made first, and the veterinarian has to know the weight, breed, and condition of the rabbit before he decides on medication and dosage.

Thoroughly clean and disinfect the cage and run. The excrement should not be used as fertilizer for raising more rabbit food because some coccidia can survive 18 months and withstand temperatures lower than −50° F.

Internal Parasites are not uncommon in rabbits. If you want to be on the safe side, have your rabbit's stool examined twice per year.

Infestation with *tapeworm larvae* can be avoided by worming your dog regularly. This is advisable for your sake as well because people are susceptible to tapeworms, too. Avoid picking greens from areas frequented by dogs. If you have a cat, have it wormed, too, even though cat tapeworm is rare in rabbits and not a danger for humans.

Infectious Respiratory Diseases (Snuffles) readily attack animals that are not properly cared for. The actual cause of these illnesses is usually the bacterium pasteurella, but a diet deficient in vitamins, too close quarters, lack of fresh air, and exposure to heat and drafts make animals more susceptible to it.

Symptoms: With snuffles, the animals sneeze, cough, and show nasal and/or ocular discharges. They may also be listless and refuse food. The disease may become localized as *eye inflammation* (conjunctivitis) or as a *middle or inner-ear infection* (otitis media). This latter inflammation cannot be seen but is signalled by a tilting of the head to one side. Pasteurella can also cause *abcesses* usually found around the neck and chin. If the disease takes the form of

When Your Rabbit Is Sick

pneumonia, there will usually be a clear nasal discharge and, frequently, circulatory problems. *Septicemia* is the generalized form of the disease and is evidenced by fever, dehydration, and weight loss.

Treatment: At the first sign of any of these symptoms, the animals should be promptly taken to a veterinarian. Pasteurella infections require professional attention and can be fatal if left untreated.

Ear Mites are parasites that settle in the ear. If neglected, they can cause much damage and discomfort. If you buy a rabbit with clean ears and if you keep your rabbit's quarters clean, the problem is unlikely to develop.

Symptoms: Head tilted to one side; drooping ears; head shaking; scratching or rubbing against furniture or cage. The diagnosis is confirmed if you see bloody, crusty, or brownish-black deposits in the ears. A head tilt can also be a sign of snuffles, but with that disease the ears will be clean.

Treatment: First, clean the cage or hutch thoroughly and change the bedding. If the ear deposits look soft, clean the inside of the ear with cotton. If the deposits are hard and crusty, use an eye dropper or a teaspoon to put 3–10 drops of *mineral oil* in the ear to wet the crusty areas.

Wait a few hours until the oil has softened the crust, then wipe the crust out. Do not use Q-tips or other hard instruments. Reach into the ear only as far as your finger will easily go. After cleaning the ear, drop 2–3 more drops as deep into the ear as you can. Repeat the entire procedure 1–3 days later and again one week later. For the next 4–5 weeks, place 2 drops of mineral oil in *both* of your rabbit's ears every week, then once every month or every other month even if there are no symptoms. Mites can still be present when there is no visible sign of them. Old and weak rabbits are particularly susceptible to ear mites.

Myxomatosis is a viral disease of rabbits that has received considerable public attention. It is transmitted by insect bites and was first observed in South America in 1898. In 1950 and 1951, Australia used this virus to fight its rabbit overpopulation. In 1952, the disease reached Europe where it wiped out wild rabbits in many areas and caused massive fatalities in domestic rabbit colonies.

Symptoms: Teary eyes, swellings on the sides of the head, and general weight loss.

Treatment: There is no treatment available yet, and vaccination is of questionable value. However, one of

When Your Rabbit Is Sick

the myxomatosis viruses is less virulent than others, and with good care some rabbits can survive. Immunity will be passed on to the offspring after recovery from the disease.

Tularemia was originally reported in Tulare County, California, hence the name tularemia. It is a disease of rodents that is transmitted by ticks and is rarely seen in rabbits. It is mentioned only because it affects dogs and people also and must be reported to public health authorities when diagnosed.

Symptoms: The disease may take the form of an acute general infection with slight fever (103–104°F) (101–102° is normal), spasms, weight loss, ruffled coat, sneezing, and weakness. You can measure your rabbit's temperature rectally with a children's thermometer. Lubricate the thermometer with Vaseline before insertion and keep it in the rectum for 2 minutes.

Treatment: There is no treatment for tularemia in rabbits.

Mange is caused by ectoparasites. It is a sign of seriously deficient sanitation.

Symptoms: The parasites bite their way into the bridge of the nose, the forehead, the base of the ears, and along the lips. They deposit their eggs there and cause patchy hair loss and scabs.

Treatment: Separate the affected animal immediately. Clean the hutch thoroughly. Soften and remove scabs with soapy water. Clip encrusted hairs away from affected areas. Ask your veterinarian to prescribe a topical mange medication that is safe for rabbits. You must begin treatment immediately to prevent the organisms from migrating into the inner ear or brain, at which point it is too late for treatment. Mange is very rare in clean rabbits.

Hair loss can be caused by nutritional deficiencies.

Heatstroke can cause sudden death in rabbits that are exposed to excessive heat without access to shade and water.

43

When Your Rabbit Is Sick

Symptoms before collapse: shallow, rapid breathing; the entire body heaves with the increased effort.

Treatment: Remove the rabbit immediately to a cooler but not cold area. Offer water at room temperature, and let the animal move about freely.

Fractures can occur if a rabbit jumps from its cage and catches a leg in the grating, if it jumps out of your arms, or if it falls from an elevated place. Rabbits that run free in your apartment can be stepped on or caught in doors. Accidents of this kind can result in spinal injuries and paralysis.

Symptoms: The animal will favor an injured limb.

Treatment: Nothing can be done for compound fractures (i.e., if the broken ends of the bone protrude through the skin). Ask for fast and effective euthanasia.

For simple fractures the veterinarian can apply a cast or splint to keep the limb immobile and allow healing. The bandaging should be covered with pine tar to keep the rabbit from chewing it off.

Hairline fractures will heal by themselves if the rabbit is kept quiet and is well cared for.

Eye Inflammations are caused by drafts, colds, dust, and excessive ammonia content in dirty bedding. Sometimes injuries from fighting can be the cause.

Symptoms: The eyes tear and are often kept closed. The conjunctivas may be red and swollen. The cornea will appear reddish or yellowish.

Treatment: Remove the cause, and get an appropriate ophthalmic ointment from your veterinarian or pet store.

A Medicine Cabinet for the Rabbit Owner

The items listed here are for minor ailments only and are not meant as a substitute for veterinary care.

Disinfectants

There are many excellent and ecologically safe disinfectants available in supermarkets and pet stores. Every three months at least you should disinfect your rabbit's quarters. Scrub everything with hot water and detergent, then follow up with a disinfectant. A thorough cleaning like this is especially important any time your rabbit has had some type of illness, particularly diarrhea.

Camomile Tea

This herbal tea can be used to wash wounds and minor injuries and irritations of the eyes. Apply with cotton, and make sure no lint is left in eyes or wounds.

Sage Tea

This herbal tea is good for swollen or inflamed mucosal lining inside the mouth. If you grow sage in your garden you can give your rabbit fresh leaves to chew on. But use only the herbal variety (*Salvia oficinalis*), not one of the ornamental types.

Peppermint Tea

Peppermint is good for indigestion and helps with diarrhea that may follow on intestinal troubles. Rabbits like to eat small amounts of peppermint leaves, which probably aid the digestion.

Linseed and Linseed Oil

Linseed tea or a teaspoon full of linseed oil is helpful for constipation. It is a bad sign if your rabbit does not pass any fecal matter for 24 hours. The underlying cause of the constipation (see page 40) should first be removed; then the linseed oil or tea will be a good supportive treatment.

Supplemental Vitamins and Minerals

Young rabbits may require supplemental vitamins and minerals during the winter months. Pregnant or nursing does always require food supplements. A veterinarian can give you the correct vitamin combination for your rabbit's size, weight, breed, and general condition. Many pet stores have well-informed personnel who can also advise you and give you appropriate references in books or rabbit journals.

Rabbit Care During Vacations

Vacations are usually planned months in advance, and it is wise to plan ahead for your rabbit's vacation care, too.

Day Trips do not require special arrangements. Leave adequate food, and do not place the cage where direct sunlight will hit it. Many rabbit owners have left their animals to a painful death by giving their rabbits "a chance to enjoy the beautiful weather."

Vacation Care should be arranged early if you plan to be away for days or weeks at a time.
• Will friends care for the rabbit in your home?
• Will friends care for it in their home?
• Will a pet store or animal hotel board your rabbit?
• Are you planning to take your rabbit with you on vacation? The first two options are the best, but you may not have reliable, animal-loving friends available when you need them.

You should use a pet store only if you know the management well and know that the shop does not become overcrowded with "boarders" during peak vacation times.

Animal hotels are not always readily available. This makes it essen-tial to plan ahead if you want to use such a facility. You should also inspect any facility where you are planning to leave your rabbit.

Most pet care facilities have reasonable prices. However, it is wise to establish what the cost will be before you make a reservation.

Hotels, Motels, or Private Lodging
If you decide to take your rabbit along on your vacation, you will have to select your own overnight quarters accordingly. In hotels and motels you are sure to encounter problems. Private lodgings, such as tourist homes, and condo rentals are likely to be more hospitable to your rabbit. If you can inspect the place beforehand, all the better. A room without carpets and wallpaper is best. You can manage with them, too, but your rabbit will have to spend more time in its cage. This is all right if you take your rabbit for half-hour walks 2 or 3 times a day in a grassy area.

You might think a vacation on a ranch or farm would be ideal; but, unfortunately, the separation between animals and people is often stricter in such places than elsewhere. I speak from experience. When we spent a vacation on a farm, it was all I could do to convince the farmer's wife that rabbits indoors did not necessarily mean stench and dirt. And indeed she

Rabbit Care During Vacations

had to admit she could not smell the rabbit, nor could she find a wisp of hay on the floor. I had brought along my own broom and dustpan; and we routinely change the litter twice a day when the rabbit has to spend a lot of time in the cage.

The leash and harness are essential on vacations. You will certainly need them the first few days when the territory is still unfamiliar, and you may well need them the whole time if there are roads or dogs nearby. Never let your rabbit run without super-vision unless it is safe behind a tight fence at least 3 feet high. Better yet is a run covered on top to keep out dogs, cats and other predators.

Be sure to take along food bowls and the food pellets you usually use at home.

Trips Abroad

If you intend to take your rabbit to a foreign country, you should call or visit the consulate in question to find out the pertinent regulations. If you fail to do this, you may be turned away at the border.

Car or Train Travel

Traveling by car or train is stressful for rabbits. The strange environment, the noise and vibration, and, often, the increased heat add to the strain. Try to make things as easy for your

rabbit as you can. The carrier (a basket or solid carton, *not* a plastic container) should lock securely, have one or two vent holes, and have a layer of newspapers, diaper cloth, or toweling on the floor. The carrier should be large enough to let the rabbit stretch out and sit up in it. If it is too large, the animal will be thrown about in it. In car travel, a passenger in the back seat should take the rabbit carrier on his or her lap. Do not put the carrier near the engine, where the animal will be too warm; and do not put it in a drafty area.

A carrier for visits to the veterinarian or for short trips.

Water should be given every two hours. When you travel by car, you can water your animal when you make your own regular rest stops. Take the rabbit out of the car and let it graze if you make a stop in the open.

Rabbit Breeding and Production

Breeding rabbits for show or production requires special knowledge, ample space, and time. An apartment or balcony is not adequate for these hobbies.

Even if you have a large yard, space for runs, and ample housing for young animals, all your problems are still not solved. Pregnant and nursing does need quiet and understanding care if all is to go well.

Also, what is to become of your young rabbits when they leave their mother after six or eight weeks and need their own housing? Will you be able to find good homes for them?

After you have solved the practical problems, I would suggest that you then become familiar with the theoretical aspects of rabbit breeding. The following short chapter is only an introduction. Sources of detailed information are given at the end of this book (page 67).

Breeder or Producer

Have you decided whether you want to breed rabbits to association standards or whether you simply want to increase numbers?

A *breeder* carefully selects breeding stock according to accepted standards for a specific strain. Some breeders also aim to develop new strains or new color combinations. These are tricky tasks! Much is being done these days with the coloration of dwarf breeds. You can, for instance, get Dwarf Angora rabbits; but since they are not yet firmly established as a standard purebred line, they have not yet been recognized as a new dwarf breed. If you want to be a serious breeder, you should become a member of a local or state breeders' association. You can find addresses through pet stores and journals, and the associations will supply you with reference material. Seminars and meetings with experienced breeders are also helpful. Finally, the associations will help you find the kind of animals you are looking for.

Rabbit *producers* breed rabbits only to multiply them. They do not need to be familiar with strain standards and other guidelines. Parents do not even have to be of the same breed. The buck may be smaller than the doe, but not vice versa. If the buck is larger, the young may be too large and complicate the birth. A too large or too heavy buck may also hurt the doe during mating.

Essential Information for Breeders and Producers

When to Breed

Young animals must be separated by sex at the age of 10–12 weeks. Soon after that, they will be sexually mature. Bucks should be placed in single cages. Female siblings that are used to each other can be housed in pairs or threes.

A buck and doe are brought together for mating at about six months of age or preferably a little later. Only then are they strong enough for breeding. Does that are bred too early may incur permanent damage.

Both animals should be in perfect health and not be shedding when they are mated.

It is best to move the doe into a large birthing and nursing hutch well before breeding and pregnancy so that she will be well adjusted to these new quarters. She should be alone in this hutch.

Mating

The female is always brought to the male. In her own quarters a doe can be quite aggressive, intimidating a male and even injuring him seriously. The buck feels more secure in his own cage. But even there a doe may initially resist or even attack the male, particularly if she does not know him. The buck, however, will not get upset or fight back. Instead he will try to avoid her bites and counter by licking and nuzzling her. He will generally succeed in calming her soon. When the buck mates with the doe, he usually has his front paws, chest, and belly on her back for a few seconds. The act is completed when he slides off her back to one side and remains motionless for a few moments. Young, inexperienced bucks may not immediately learn how to handle a doe, even in their own cages. In such cases, you should allow a few weeks to pass before bringing the pair together again. There are rare occasions where a female will simply refuse to tolerate a certain male. Rabbits too have their likes and dislikes.

The breeder stays with the rabbits during mating. After the procedure, the female is taken back to her cage. If the mating was successful the doe will show signs of nervous or agitated scratching a few days after the mating.

Caring for the Pregnant Doe

During pregnancy the doe needs peace and quiet. Keep her hutch in its usual place, and do not alter the hutch itself or its environment. The presence of strangers can be upsetting to her.

A tame animal will still enjoy being petted, but you should not pick it up or carry it around. If you must carry or lift the doe, remember to support the hindquarters carefully. Do not lift her by the scruff of her neck alone.

Diet for the Pregnant Doe

A pregnant doe should get, in addition to the usual varied diet, some

Rabbit Breeding and Production

oats, a calcium supplement, and/or a mineral/vitamin supplement every day. Additional greens are also a good idea. Incorrect or deficient diet during pregnancy has often been cited as a reason for inadequate mothering behavior after giving birth.

Does kept outdoors should get additional drinking water. During warm weather a bottle with a sipper tube can be used. During the winter months, provide a bowl filled with water at room temperature. A rabbit will drink enough water for the needs of one whole day in just ten to fifteen minutes. Then remove the bowl to prevent the water from cooling too much.

Nesting and Birth

During her pregnancy of 28–31 days, the doe will need extra straw or hay in her hutch. About one week before the young are due to be born, the doe will build a nest with hay. She will line that nest with tufts of her own fur. This soft bed will provide a warm nursery for the baby rabbits that are born blind and hairless.

One or two days after the babies are born (you will be able to tell because the doe will be slim again), you should check the nest. A normally tame doe will let you pet it with one hand while you check the nest with the other. Remove any dead animals and leave the healthy ones alone.

If your doe is very nervous, take her out of the cage while you check the baby rabbits in the nest. Then return the mother, and give her some favorite nibbles as a reward.

Nursing

For 3 weeks the babies depend completely on their mother's milk for food. Soon thereafter they start nibbling on their mother's food and increase their intake of it continuously. At about 6 weeks after birth, they will be completely weaned.

Diet for the Nursing Doe

Feed the same diet as during pregnancy, but offer food three times every day. Remember the additional drinking water; it is essential now.

How Many Litters per Year

The average number of babies is six, but Dwarf Albinos usually have only two or three. Pregnancy and nursing are quite strenuous for a doe, and you should not let her have more than 3 litters per year.

If a Nursing Doe Dies

If the mother rabbit dies within the first weeks after delivery, caring for the orphaned rabbits will require much effort and attention, but it can be done. I personally know a family that raised 4 baby rabbits whose mother died when they were 10 days old.

50

Rabbit Breeding and Production

The recommended diet is baby formula, which you can feed with an eye dropper available from any drugstore.

The formula must be mixed fresh at each feeding and be at body temperature. Depending on the age, condition, and appetite of the babies, you can feed them 3–6 times per day. (Baby rabbits need to drink only once or twice from their mother to take in enough milk for a whole day.) When the rabbits are quietly asleep and have rounded bellies, they have had enough milk. After feeding them, you can stroke their bellies gently to stimulate digestion and elimination. The mother does this with vigorous licking.

The babies have to be kept warm during the first 3 weeks. If it is cool, fill a hot water bottle with warm water, wrap a towel around it, and place it under the nest. Refill with warm water as needed. Keep all bedding meticulously clean.

The friends I mentioned above began raising their baby rabbits indoors, but once the babies were able to eat and drink on their own, my friends put them—as an experiment only—in a hutch with their father because it was too cold outdoors for them to be alone. Despite the bad name that bucks have as uncaring fathers, this one was a model parent. He licked his children, warmed them, and even let them eat his food. When the babies had to be separated from him, he grieved for days on end. Another experience my friends had also proves that bucks are better fathers than they are thought to be. Being inexperienced with rabbits my friends had left a male and a female together and had not noticed that the doe was pregnant. They became aware of the babies only hours after the youngsters had been born. Although the buck was present during the birth and nursing, there was no fighting, biting, or commotion. This goes to show that domestic bucks are as good fathers as their brothers in the wild.

Understanding Rabbits

Most of us will come to understand animals if we are exposed to them over a long period of time and watch them carefully. We will understand them both as individuals and as members of their species. And each animal *is* an individual. No two dogs, cats, rabbits, or guinea pigs are exactly the same. They vary in their capacity to learn as well as in the way they respond to people they know. But it is helpful if you are familiar with typical behavior patterns and can correctly interpret signs your rabbit gives you. This chapter is designed to help you do this.

Rabbit Language

Rabbits can communicate with us, even though they are capable of only a few sounds that are almost inaudible for us. They also communicate with body language, conveying a variety of moods very effectively.

Sounds

Growling: The short, almost barklike growl indicates an aggressive mood usually provoked by an assumed attack. Caution! This growl may precede a bite. Perhaps you have handled your animal incorrectly.

You override the animal's wishes only if its welfare is at stake. Our Titus has to spend the night in his box during the winter months because the floor is too cold for him and has made him sick in the past. However, he is otherwise used to complete freedom of movement; and, come winter time, he makes it clear to us that he objects to the box. He growls but gradually adjusts to the winter routine.

Low Squealing: You will hear this sound only if you are close by. Most rabbits use it to indicate that they want to be put down and allowed to run free.

Gnashing the Teeth: Most rabbits I know gnash their teeth slowly and with what appears to be great pleasure when they are being petted. They usually stretch out at their ease and seem to be completely relaxed when making this sound.

"Purring": Sustained low purring sounds indicate a willingness on the part of the buck to court and mate. He will usually circle the doe while he makes these sounds. However, a buck periodically feels like mating even in the absence of a doe. He expresses this by circling familiar humans and by collecting twigs, leaves, and scraps of paper. Perhaps this is the way that bucks in the wild help their mates with nest building. When our Titus is in this mood he often circles a ball

A mother with her litter at feeding time. These are ▷ small German Lops.

about the size of a rabbit, pushes it in front of him, licks it, and occasionally tries to mount it. But he will instantly forget the ball if a female appears.

Tapping: Rabbits tap or beat with their hind legs when they are frightened. Their eyes become enlarged, and they immediately run for cover. Titus appears to interpret our neighbor's rug beating as an urgent warning.

Body Language

A tense body and upright tail indicate excitement. If, in addition, the ears are laid back, the rabbit may be about to attack. Two bucks will assume this posture when about to fight over territory. For your domestic rabbit, this territory may include just the room or balcony where his cage is kept, your whole apartment, or the entire yard, depending on how much freedom of movement he is used to.

A tense sitting position with ears laid back means that he is ready to defend himself. As with wild rabbits, his weapons of defense are the claws on his front paws. These claws are hard but not sharp.

Rubbing with the underside of the chin on all kinds of objects, e.g., plants, stairs, etc. (usually done by males, less by females) indicates that the rabbit considers these things part of his territory.

Nudging with the muzzle means that your rabbit wants attention.

"Digging" on blankets and carpeting also means he wants some petting and will stop as soon as you comply.

If your rabbit licks you, that is his appreciative response to being petted. This "social grooming" is always a sure sign of affection toward you, just as it is toward other animals.

If your rabbit pushes your hand away with his nose, he has had all the petting he wants for the moment.

If a pet rabbit raises himself on his hind legs, he wants to get a better view of something. Sometimes he does this at doors or gates to tell you that he wants to come in or go out.

If he lays back his ears and stretches out on his belly with his eyes half shut, he needs rest and sleep. If

A rabbit's attack stance. Other house pets, such as dogs and cats, have a different body language.

Understanding Rabbits

it is cool, a rabbit pulls his front paws in under his body before going to sleep.

Resting posture. When your rabbit lies down like this, it wants to be left alone.

Rolling over on the back is a sign of sheer delight.

Rolling on his sides or back indicates a sense of extreme well-being.

Rabbits enjoy participating in all activities that take place at their own level, probably because they like company and like to keep busy.

When we weed our garden, for example, Titus will hurry from one to the other of us to snitch samples from the weed baskets. When we trim our shrubs, he will carry small twigs around; and when we do any digging we have to be careful not to trip over him.

Whenever our children play games on the floor, he will join them and move the pieces of a board game around, or he may disappear with dice or cards. When we clean out drawers, he will quickly jump into one of them and "help" by shredding notebooks and papers. But who could possibly get mad at him?

What You Should Know about Rabbits in the Wild

You know by now that domestic rabbits are descended from wild rabbits. Like all domestic animals that have been raised by man for generations and that are not threatened by enemies or forced to search for their own food, domestic rabbits are more delicate, have less stamina, and are less hardy than their relatives in the wild. Their hearts, for example, are weaker than those of wild rabbits.

Still, the behavior patterns of domestic rabbits are similar to those of wild rabbits. The behavior typical of the species has evolved over a long

Understanding Rabbits

period of time and in response to the demands of survival. This behavior is so deeply ingrained that no amount of training can remove it.

If you know something about the life of a wild rabbit, you will understand your pet rabbit better and will be able to provide him with the living conditions best suited to his nature. Also, you will not be as likely to think of your rabbit as boring or stupid, and you and he will live together in mutual enjoyment and contentment. This is why I want to tell you a little about wild rabbits.

What Wild Rabbits Look Like

Wild rabbits weigh 2–4 pounds and are 13–17 inches long. Their ears are about 2¾ inches long. The head, body, and legs are shorter and stockier than a hare's. Their fur is brownish gray with touches of reddish ochre in the neck area and grayish white on the belly. This coloration provides wild rabbits with excellent camouflage.

Pet rabbits will occasionally behave as if they had this camouflage even though they do not. Our white rabbit Caesar used to play dead in a freshly plowed field when he saw the silhouette of a "bird of prey," actually a small airplane, above him. Since there was no cover near by, he relied on camouflage he did not have.

Where Wild Rabbits Live

Wild rabbits can be found in many parts of the world, but they do not thrive in wet and rainy climates or harsh winters, nor do they live at altitudes above 2,000 feet (600m). They prefer a light sandy soil to a heavy clay soil and like pine growth with plenty of underbrush. However, they can adapt to less favorable conditions.

Rabbits dig burrows with several shafts and tunnels and a den. They dig with their powerful front legs and use their hind legs to push back the dirt. If they hit a major obstruction, they change the direction of their tunneling or start fresh somewhere else.

Pet rabbits like to dig, too. If they have little opportunity to dig outdoors, they will go through the motions of digging inside.

Territory

The territory extends out from the den in a radius of about 600 yards (600 m), taking in about 50 acres. This area is not always completely utilized because there is often ample food near the den, and the proximity of the den represents security. If danger threatens, the animals are usually near one of the entrances to the burrow. (One study showed that one particular territory had five times as many entrances to the burrow as there were rabbits.)

Understanding Rabbits

Domestic rabbits retain an excellent sense of direction and quickly learn where gates and doors are. However, they need adequate time to explore an unfamiliar environment. Domestic rabbits, like their cousins in the wild, are very cautious when exposed to new surroundings. They stretch out their necks, sniff with a rapidly twitching nose, and forget about food, even if you place a great delicacy in front of them.

If a rabbit exploring new territory meets another rabbit on its turf, the newcomer will flee rather than fight, even if the "local" rabbit is not yet full grown. This remains true even with animals that are quite sure of themselves in their familiar environment.

Rabbits mark their territory by rubbing the scent glands in their chins against objects.

Because of this it is best not to take a rabbit for a walk as you would a dog; nor should you take him on a trip where you expect to see many new things. For a rabbit that means nothing but fear and stress.

Take your rabbit only to places where you will stay for several hours: a garden, a park, a meadow, or a vacation spot with ample opportunity for runs. If the area is not fenced, use the leash, letting your rabbit lead you. Truly tame and properly handled animals will not try to escape, but dogs always present a danger.

Wild rabbits establish runways in their territory, and these paths are used over and over again. Feces and urine are deposited at specific locations, often on top of abandoned mole hills.

Domestic rabbits, too, quickly establish a network of paths within their territory and will use specific spots to relieve themselves. They mark their territory and its borders by distributing specific scents. Every rabbit is equipped with anal glands that give off a special scent and that are used to impregnate the feces with this odor while the feces are still in the intestine. These feces that mark territory are easily distinguishable from regular feces even for our noses. Wild rabbits mark the borders of their territory by dropping small piles of these feces. Other rabbits then know that a particular territory is already occupied.

To mark specific spots or objects, such as tree stumps, rocks, branches, or bushes, a rabbit will rub them with his chin. Special secretions from glands under the chin give off a scent that is not detectable by humans. Bucks use these glandular secretions to mark the entrances to their burrows, their females and young, and the feces of other rabbits.

The Social Order

Rabbits live in groups. Even if only a single pair of rabbits settles in one particular area, a colony will soon develop. Does have several litters during the summer months. The young usually leave their home territory when they reach maturity, but a few settle there. Young animals from

When rabbits meet, they touch noses and determine by scent if they will take to each other.

other territories may also join the colony. In this way, the colony's growth is assured.

All the animals get to know each other and can tell each other apart. The glandular secretions described above play a major role here. By sniffing places and objects marked by other animals, rabbits can recognize the age and gender of the rabbit that made the markings and tell whether the animal belongs to their own group or another one. They can even tell whether a doe is tending her young or not.

This explains why rabbits, including domestic ones, always spend a lot of time sniffing another rabbit's feces as well as the markings it has made with its chin glands. Even if the originator of these markings is close by, other rabbits will examine the markings first before turning to the animal itself.

Feces from intruders are immediately recognized and "treated" with scent from the chin glands. In this way, established rabbits substitute their own scent for that of the intruder.

Bucks are equipped with larger anal and chin glands than are does. But the size and capacity of these glands varies in individuals, too. We know that animals with large glands always hold high rankings in their group. Also, if two males that do not know each other are put together, the male that uses his chin glands the most is quickly accepted as superior by the other.

Bucks frequently use not only their chin glands but also spray urine to mark their group.

If an adult male intrudes, all the established males and especially the highest ranking buck in a colony will fight him off fiercely and drive him away. Bucks fight by using their claws, by biting, and by spraying urine.

Male domestic rabbits behave similarly toward strange males. They even attack familiar bucks at mating time or to defend their territory, thus reaffirming previously established rankings. The urine used in fighting smells very strong and is reddish in color. Rabbit urine is ordinarily light yellow.

Females can always count on a friendly welcome. However, they had better avoid the mate of the highest ranking buck.

Young animals, including young bucks, are welcome, too. They are considered "children," and everyone behaves in a friendly manner. The adult rabbits within the territory spray newcomers with urine and so mark them as belonging to the group. (This is not common among domestic rabbits.) When the young males have reached adulthood, they will be tolerated within the colony only if they show deference to "the boss" by making way for him whenever they meet him.

Young males, too, establish a ranking order, usually by rough play.

Young adult bucks pair up with females that are sometimes "live-ins" of the highest ranking buck, and in this way they increase the size of the colony.

Rabbits treat their young, their mates, and their siblings in a friendly and gentle manner. Roughness and fighting occur only among rivals. It is perhaps for this reason that domestic rabbits tend to interpret any roughhousing and teasing as an act of aggression and react by biting. Their biting can range from a warning nip to a firm, powerful bite that can draw blood.

Pairing

Rabbits are monogamous by nature. Couples sleep together in their burrow, graze together, and treat each other considerately. Sometimes the buck will mate with other does, but those does live in their own dens, never with the buck and his "wife." Paired does avoid other bucks and will even fight them off vigorously with their paws. Bucks

Understanding Rabbits

Relaxed and stretched out in this position the rabbit is about to go to sleep.

behave quite chivalrously with does, and will not strike back even if attacked by them.

The pairing season for wild rabbits is from late winter to midsummer. During this time, the marking glands are very active because reproduction makes territorial marking and defense particularly important. Pairing in domestic rabbits is not as closely linked to the seasons, and offspring may be born in mid-winter. But domestic rabbits will be more active sexually in the spring and summer, too, and will do much chin marking during that time. Even in the absence of does, bucks will still fight. In the summer we cannot put our buck Titus in the yard together with our friends' buck Candy, or they might hurt each other seriously. In the winter, however, Titus does not bother his smaller rival much; and if he does, Candy gives way to him. When a wild buck courts a doe, he follows her for a while, keeping his distance and performing odd little leaps. His tail stands straight up, as it does whenever he is excited. If the two take to each other, they may spend up to half an hour lying nose to nose, licking each other's head and ears. If domestic rabbits were left to themselves long enough, they would probably behave similarly.

Offspring

The baby rabbits are born 28–31 days after mating. Several days prior to parturition, the doe will dig a special shaft in the burrow with a breeding den at the end of it. She lines this den with dry grass, moss, and fur from her belly. As the young are born, the doe eats the placenta and membranes and severs the umbilical cord. The baby rabbits need a warm nest, for they are born hairless and weigh just under 2 ounces. They are also blind and deaf.

The mother nurses and cleans her babies twice daily. When she leaves the den, she carefully blocks the entrance to it with dirt to keep out enemies and the cold. She marks the entrance with urine and droppings to warn other rabbits not to scratch or dig here. The young develop quickly. At 8 days they have a furry coat, can crawl about the nest, and respond to sound. At 10 days their eyes open.

At about 3 weeks of age they weigh 5–5½ ounces and are ready to leave the nest. At this time the father begins to take notice of them. He cleans them, takes them out grazing, and warns them of danger. They can soon eat adult food, and by 4 or 5 weeks they no longer need mother's milk.

Soon they are completely independent, but wild rabbits are not sexually mature until they are 8–10 months old.

Domestic baby rabbits need their mothers a little longer, and domestic rabbit fathers are much better than they are reputed to be.

Food and Foraging

Wild rabbits are choosy if a wide variety of food is available, and they will avoid poisonous plants. Domestic rabbits are gourmets, too; but I would not rely on their ability to avoid such plants.

Wild rabbits are often forced to feed on the bark of trees and bushes during the harsh winter months. Domestic rabbits, too, like the bark of young twigs, and they retain the art of stripping bark, practicing it often on wallpaper and book bindings.

Rabbits need hard foods (twigs, carrots, kohlrabi, cauliflower, lettuce stems) to nibble on because their teeth continue to grow all the time and need to be worn down.

Wild rabbits living in populated areas go foraging mainly in the evening and at night. In rainy, windy, or snowy weather they prefer to stay in their burrows, sometimes for days on end. During these times they presumably live on roots, a food our domestic rabbits like too.

"Digestive Pills": Wild and domestic rabbits regularly eat some of their feces immediately after dropping them. Important vitamins (B complex, K, etc.) formed in the appendix are contained in the feces. When this fecal intake was withdrawn in experiments, the animals became weak and sickly.

Rabbits keep healthy by eating some of their own fresh droppings.

Getting Comfortable

To the best of my knowledge wild rabbits sleep on the bare floors of their dens. Do they scratch around before they lie down? I suppose so, since even domestic rabbits do that in their nests. They need bedding to stay healthy, and they appreciate warm, soft blankets or rugs.

Wild rabbits do a lot of grooming and keep very clean. If they have to be outside in rainy weather, they shake their paws frequently. They obviously dislike being wet and muddy. The same is true of domestic rabbits.

Capabilities of the Senses

Wild rabbits have better vision than hares, but even for them hearing is more important. The ears are almost always on the alert. The sense of smell is highly developed, too. The blunt nose is constantly in motion and can be twisted about in a comical fashion, sometimes looking quite cockeyed, as it studies an interesting scent. Sitting up on their hind legs gives rabbits a better vantage for seeing, smelling, and orienting themselves.

Domestic rabbits hear better than they see, too, and have a fine sense of smell. They recognize individual people and other pets by scent and voice. Titus will sometimes attack our old cat Beppi, mistaking him for Putti; but then he stops dead in his tracks when he is close enough to smell that it is indeed Beppi. Titus clearly cannot distinguish their shapes even though Putti is significantly larger.

Escaping from Enemies

Wild rabbits avoid predators by rapid flight. Foxes, weasels, martens, and hawks hunt adult rabbits; weasels and owls pursue the young. The most dangerous enemies, however, are men and dogs.

At the slightest sign of danger wild rabbits drum with their hind legs, warning other rabbits in that area. Wild rabbits are faster and more agile than hares, although they cannot jump as high or as far. They are also masters of feinting and dodging and can quickly disappear into burrows or under thick, thorny bushes. In open fields they may choose to play dead, relying on their coloration to camouflage them.

Flight is natural to domestic rabbits, too. Even your pet rabbit will run if you try to catch him. He, too, is a master of broken-field running. Patience, standing still, and calling are therefore usually more productive than wild chases and will spare your nerves as well as your rabbit's. If you use the same words and intonation consistently, you can be quite sure of success.

Understanding Rabbits

If you feed dry pellets only in the house, you can use reward feeding as an incentive for obedience. However, do not expect a rabbit to obey your call instantly the way a dog does. Rabbits need more time, and impatience can spoil everything.

A young rabbit owner I know uses this "confusion trick": He runs tight circles around his rabbit, then grabs it quickly and firmly without hurting it.

Our call "Titus, come here!" is obeyed immediately when Titus feels like obeying. It is obeyed more slowly when he prefers to remain outside; and we are totally ignored when he has been out only a short while. We can tell, though, by the twitching of his ears that he has heard us call. We resort to the leash and harness if we have only a short time to walk him.

I hope you now have some sense of rabbit nature, of wild rabbits' complicated yet smoothly functioning social life, and of their natural environment.

You are now familiar with the various means of expression rabbits have to convey their moods and wishes. This will help you to deal properly with your rabbit, whose environment you determine and for whom you take the place of fellow creatures.

Appendix

Books and Addresses for Further Information

1. *Official Guide to Raising Better Rabbits*
   The American Rabbit Breeders Association
   1925 South Main, Box 426
   Bloomington, IL 81701
2. *Domestic Rabbit Biology and Production*
   L. R. Arrington and Kathleen Kelley:
   University Presses of Florida
3. *Nutrient Requirements of Rabbits*
   Committee on Animal Nutrition:
   National Academy Press
4. *How to Raise Rabbits for Fun and Profit*
   Milton I. Faivre: Nelson-Hall, Inc.
5. *The Wild Rabbit*
   Oxford Scientific Films: G. P. Putnam's & Sons
6. *Encyclopedia of Pet Rabbits*
   David Robinson: T.F.H. Publications
7. *Rabbits and Other Small Animals*
   Time-Life Television Editors:
   Time-Life Books

List of American Rabbit Breeds

American Checkered Giant
American Dutch (Black, Blue, Chocolate, Tortoise, Grey)
American White, Blue, Sable, Chinchilla
Belgian Hare
Beveren's (White, Blue, Black)
Californian
Champagne D'Argent
Creme D'Argent
English Angora (White, Black, Blue, Fawn)
English Spots (Blue, Black, Chocolate, Grey, Tortoise, Lilac)
Flemish Giants (Grey, Sandy, Black, Blue, White, Fawn)
Florida White
French Angora (White, Black, Blue, Fawn)
Harlequin
Havanna (Brown, Blue)
Himalayan
Lilac
Lops (French, English, Varied, White)
New Zealand (Red, White, Black)
Palomino (Golden, Lynx)
Polish (White, Black, Chocolate)
Rex (White, Black, Blue, Castor, Chinchilla, Opal, Lynx, Sable, Seal, Red, Lilac, Havanna, California)
Satin (Black, Blue, Havanna, Red, Chinch, Copper, Siamese)
Siamese Sable
Silver Fox (Blue, Black)
Silver Martin (Blue, Black, Chocolate, Sable)
Silvers (Grey, Fawn, Brown)
Tans (Black, Blue, Chocolate, Lilac)

Index

Index